BRITAIN IN OLD PHOTOGRAPHS

MILTON KEYNES

R O B E R T   C O O K

ALAN SUTTON PUBLISHING LIMITED

Alan Sutton Publishing Limited
Phoenix Mill · Far Thrupp · Stroud
Gloucestershire · GL5 2BU

First published 1995

Cover photographs: front: Bill Billings'
dinosaur creation, Pear Tree Bridge; *back:* the
Salvation Army Corps Band, New Bradwell,
1926.

British Library Cataloguing in Publication Data.
A catalogue record for this book is available from
the British Library.

ISBN 0–7509–0837–8

Typeset in 9/10 Sabon.
Typesetting and origination by
Alan Sutton Publishing Limited.
Printed in Great Britain by
Ebenezer Baylis, Worcester.

Ray Bellchambers on the Development Corporation's tour of Japan, 1978. A ghostly
stupa (peace pagoda) dominates the background. The Corporation was planning a
similar pagoda for Milton Keynes. (Ray Bellchambers)

Contents

Introduction   5

1. All Things Bright and Beautiful   7

2. Bare Bones   24

3. Naked City Images   52

4. The Way They Were   78

    Acknowledgements   126

Local artist Bill Billings' massive train mural painted on the wall of Wolverton's historic railway works. There were 819 staff here when British Rail Maintenance sold it to the Railcare consortium in June 1995. The works will continue to house the royal train, which has been here since Queen Victoria's reign.

Introduction

My first memory of the new city of Milton Keynes was at Woughton on the Green in the summer of 1971. I crossed the little humpback bridge and gazed out wistfully at the thirteenth-century church from a Sidney Green contractor's Land Rover. I was enjoying the romance of playing the young building navvy, but I could not ignore the romance of the past which was all around me. I was a minion in an army set to change the landscape.

Combine harvesters were gathering final harvests in some of the fields, while we toiled in deep trenches laying pipes. Odd characters were all around me. One was 'Smiffy', a small Irishman aged about sixty, who had two identical mauve shirts and grey suits. He wore one lot to work and hung the other in our tea and breakfast cabin – that was his 'beering suit'. He told many tall stories when he returned from his weekends in Bletchley, opening them all with: 'Jesus Christ, I never saw anything like it in my life.'

The same might be said about me and the building of Milton Keynes. Sadly, I cannot get all of the pictures out of my head and into this collection, but I have done my best to provide a sample, along with comments linking past and present.

In spite of all the changes in the area, Milton Keynes' past is still very much in evidence. Most obviously it is preserved at the Museum of Rural Life at Stacey Bushes and through the work of the Living Archive. Then there are the place names. Shenley, meaning 'bright clearing', takes us back to Saxon times, when the lord held the manor, and farmers worked the land in strips – usually there were three large fields per parish, and crops were rotated to enrich the soil naturally. The parishes were grouped in hundreds and the rules of local government were hard and fast.

Ruling over the area were great names such as Grey, Radcliffe and Wolverton (whose prominence derived from the Norman Conquest), and life was tough for common folk. People needed strong leaders to keep them in check and to organize defences. Before the Saxons came, Queen Boudicca stormed around the region standing up to the Romans. She perished in AD 60 near the place we now call Towcester.

The Romans brought their wealth and made a famous road, Watling Street, running from London to Wroxeter. This might have been a model for 1960s planners, who did their best to reshape existing roads and build a new city centre with a linear road pattern. The new city was part of a process to create settlements around the capital, and it derived from postwar hopes to rehouse a mainly London overspill. It brought some misery to those set in their ways, but people had been uprooted before. For example, much distress had been caused in the sixteenth century when local aristocracy decided to enclose arable land in Stantonbury, Bradwell, Woughton and Tattenhoe. Some villages, including Stanton Low, were destroyed while others, such as Woughton, shrank. The common folk might have protested, but in the end they had to adjust. When plans for Milton Keynes were mooted Wolverton Urban District Council had strong objections to a scheme that would make a proud community part of a greater whole. But eventually it came round. Similarly the residents of Milton Keynes village, now part of a conservation area which includes the oldest house in the district, asked why a 25,000 acre city planned to engulf them should be named after their 'unspoilt, clean and tidy village'. Meanwhile planners talked of a 'car-free all-electric' alternative to other conurbations. 'Get on the right wave length – think of yourselves not as simply living in Bletchley, Wolverton or Stony Stratford,' said Lord Campbell of Eskan, who was chosen to lead the Development Corporation.

Where is the city now? The Commission for New Towns will shut up shop in 1998, leaving the Borough Council concerned that 25 per cent of the city will remain undeveloped. Chief Executive Michael Murray does not want the land to be sold off piecemeal. But the 1980s and '90s saw a greedy reaction to '60s planning hopes – accelerated by a change in government priorities. Milton Keynes is undoubtedly a very vital, diverse and dynamic place, in which as former Development Corporation member Ray Bellchambers commented, 'much music is made'. But there is another side to it: Police Chief Superintendent Caroline Nicholl said that reopening Central Milton Keynes Shopping Centre at night would stretch police resources too thinly and expose housing estates to greater crime. However, does that make it better or worse than any other British city? Milton Keynes may have brought great change to north Buckinghamshire, but during the past twenty-five years there have been far greater changes in the world beyond. Milton Keynes new town could not go unaffected.

Robert Cook
July 1995

The South East Economic Planning Strategy envisaged growth along existing or planned trunk roads and motorways. The M1 opened in 1959, linking London and the Midlands. It is pictured here near Wolverton in the early days. This route made north Bucks an ideal location for substantial development. The only real problem was that the land around the Rivers Ouse and Ouzel was poorly drained.

ALL THINGS BRIGHT
AND BEAUTIFUL

Doom or bloom? The village namesake signpost,
1966. The North Bucks Times *called it a*
quaint joke to name the new city after this
Domesday Book village.

Walton Hall and St Michael's Church, home of the Open University, photographed from the air, February 1972. Walton was a post-Domesday village. It was first mentioned in 1189, when the original church was built. The first known occupants were the Rixbaunds, in about 1200. The Beales are better known; a monument to Bartholomew Beale (1583–1660) and his wife Katherine was erected in the chancel of the church in 1674 by their eldest and youngest sons, Henry and Charles. The latter married Mary Craddock, the first professional female artist – she painted Charles II.

Later came the Gilpins, Pinfolds, Harleys and Earles. Dr Harley toured the area in his pony and trap. On his travels he took exception to rowdies in the Pine Tree pub, so he bought and then closed it. He died in 1923 and his eldest daughter married Brigadier Eric Earle, who won the DSO in 1914.

During the Second World War, Wrens working at Bletchley Park intelligence base occupied Walton Hall. The Earles moved into Walton Lodge Cottage. Mr Baden Powell recounts how Mrs Earle escaped from Italy the day war was declared. He notes: 'She was a lady not by title but in herself. She wouldn't pass you by without speaking. She ran the farm while the Brigadier was away and I gave her a hand at harvest.'

After the brigadier's death in 1965, the hall lay empty. The Development Corporation used it as its planning and architects' offices in 1968, before returning to Wavendon Tower in summer 1969. Meanwhile Harold Wilson planned to build on a 1920s idea to use radio for mass education. Canada, the USA and USSR were already using television for distance learning. Following an announcement in 1963 Mr Wilson appointed Arts Minister Jennie Lee to see the project through. The Open University moved into Walton Hall in September 1969, and the foundation stone was unveiled the following day. (Open University)

SOUTH EAST PLANNING REGION STRATEGY

NORTHAMPTON

IPSWICH

MILTON
KEYNES

LUTON

OXFORD

CHELMSFORD

SWINDON

READING

GREATER
LONDON

SOUTHEND

ASHFORD

CHANNEL
TUNNEL

SOUTH
HANTS

SOUTHAMPTON

HASTINGS

BRIGHTON

PORTSMOUTH

BOURNEMOUTH

FUTURE GROWTH SECTORS
STUDY AREAS
GREEN SECTORS
COUNTRY ZONES
METROPOLITAN GREEN BELT
MAJOR GROWTH POINTS

This map shows the South East Economic Planning Council's mid-1960s plan for four major swathes of development stretching away from London. The plan aimed to make the greatest use of motorways and main line railways existing or planned up to 1975. The Planning Council intended that the bulk of the region's growth should be steered into these areas and that surrounding countryside be subject to ruthless planning controls (the future turned out differently). The County Council responded with the Pooley plan.

County Council architect Fred Pooley with a model of his original plan, 1964. In November of that year North Bucks MP Robert (he liked to be known as Bob) Maxwell stated: 'From what I have been able to gather of the financial and practical feasibility of the Pooley scheme I should be surprised if the government were to decide in its favour.'

'Keep the monorail'

Pooley planned a 23,000 acre city for 250,000 inhabitants. A monorail was intended to reduce dependence on the motor car. But the city did not even get a railway station until 1982. By May 1965 the County Council abandoned the proposed partnership with the government in favour of forming a development corporation, because the government would not guarantee to make up for any shortfall of funds owing to a lack of private investment.

The County Planning Committee has emphasised to the Ministry that a monorail town on the lines already suggested is something that it believes in and which it thinks to be feasible. "The essential thing," the Committee says, "is that the town should be a credit to the County and the country."

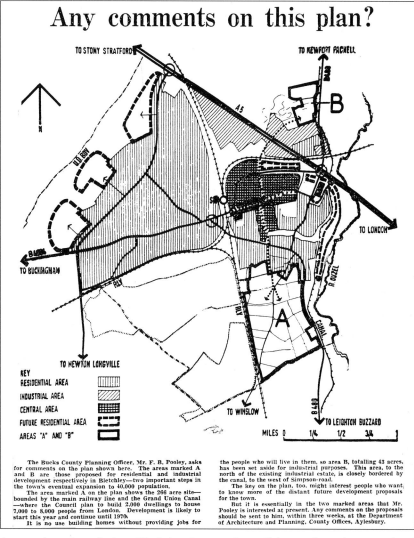

Any comments on this plan?

KEY

RESIDENTIAL AREA	
INDUSTRIAL AREA	
CENTRAL AREA	
FUTURE RESIDENTIAL AREA	
AREAS "A" AND "B"	

The Bucks County Planning Officer, Mr. F. B. Pooley, asks for comments on the plan shown here. The areas marked A and B are those proposed for residential and industrial development respectively in Bletchley—two important steps in the town's eventual expansion to 40,000 population.

The area marked A on the plan shows the 266 acre site—bounded by the main railway line and the Grand Union Canal—where the Council plan to build 2,000 dwellings to house 7,000 to 8,000 people from London. Development is likely to start this year and continue until 1970.

It is no use building homes without providing jobs for the people who will live in them, so area B, totalling 43 acres, has been set aside for industrial purposes. This area, to the north of the existing industrial estate, is closely bordered by the canal, to the west of Simpson-road.

The key on the plan, too, might interest people who want to know more of the distant future development proposals for the town.

But it is essentially in the two marked areas that Mr. Pooley is interested at present. Any comments on the proposals should be sent to him, within three weeks, at the Department of Architecture and Planning, County Offices, Aylesbury.

This was the rejected plan. Had the County Council been allowed to go ahead in partnership with private enterprise, the estimated cost would have been: site, £6 million; construction, £29 million (including £18 million for the monorail alone); this excludes the cost of 75 per cent of public sector housing (£120 million). Private enterprise was to invest £100 million. Another £40 million would have been needed for Council services. The land cost was the most uncertain. Bass Hill Farm, Nash, was the first farm to be sold in the Pooley city area, in February 1965. The *Wolverton Express* reported: 'Farmers crowded into the sale room at the Swan Hotel, Leighton Buzzard. Some were interested in buying the farm at a price. Many others were there to see how much this "city land" would fetch.' The 147½ acres sold for a handsome £34,500. The new owners were safe in the knowledge that any later compulsory purchase would be at a higher price.

Protesting north Bucks farmers wait for Local Government and Housing Minister Richard Crossman, March 1966. Posters carried such messages as 'Can't live on pills' and 'Build a city on poor land'. One plan to help displaced farmers offered them cheap land in Portugal. Clerk of the Works Brian O'Sullivan recalls of 1975: 'We were building the city centre, working on road H6. This particular farmer wouldn't go. He parked his combine harvester outside his house and we dug the land out around it while he was having his tea.'

Irene Martin and Peter Clarke, February 1967. Asked what they thought of the planned new city, Peter said: 'I think it's a shame to build on some of the best farmland in the country. It should have been built on somewhere like Dartmoor.' However, both agreed that the expansion of industry would allow young people to stay in the district.

Robert Peacock, 1967. He told interviewers that 'it was a good idea to keep the name Milton Keynes'. A farmer's son and a pupil at Radcliffe Grammar School, Wolverton, he was not keen to see the countryside go. However, he thought it better to plan a town from scratch rather than develop the established communities, because that would lead to muddle and congestion.

Bletchley councillor Jim Cassidy. He said at the time of his appointment to the Development Corporation in 1967: 'I was born in a slum (he came to Bletchley in 1950) so I know just how important it is to people to get a decent home of their own. There is no doubt that the problem of our time is housing.'

The *Daily Express* dubbed this inquiry meeting at Wilton Hall in July 1966 the 'Battle of Bletchley'. Objectors met government officials. One hundred farmers were among them. The hall was more usually used for dancing, bingo and wrestling, but this event was no fun at all. Other issues raised included the region's poor water supply and flooding; local brickmakers expressed anxieties about plans for their land.

Bob Maxwell MP, right, listens to L.E. Fairey, chairman of Olney Parish Council, at a packed meeting to discuss his town's future, January 1966. The Milton Keynes plan aspired to protect areas around the designated new city, and the meeting heard Maxwell claim that Olney could be turned into a model town without destroying a bit of its character.

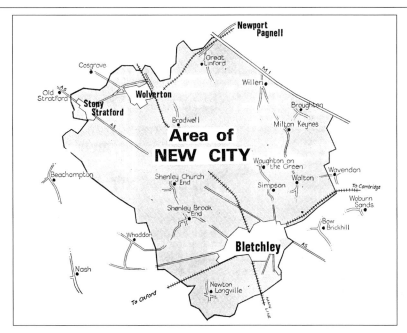

This 1966 map shows the many villages soon to be engulfed by the new city development. The Revd Mr Bromley of Broughton and Milton Keynes village gave his 'unbiased' opinion of the plan: 'I don't think the town will affect me personally, but I hope to have larger congregations.'

Milton Keynes Development Corporation was ready for business by July 1967. It chose this building, Wavendon Tower, as its headquarters. The tower was built at the turn of the century for the Revd Henry Burney as a wedding gift for his son Col. Henry Burney, who lived there until 1915. The building was an Admiralty communications centre during the Second World War. Wavendon is now best known for Johnny Dankworth's music venue, The Stables.

Farmer and Bucks county councillor T.J. Bradshaw was a leading opponent of new city plans. Unspoilt villages such as Woughton on the Green were among the most picturesque in the Home Counties. Woughton was rife with legends of Dick Turpin and, as T.J. Bradshaw pointed out, farmland was second to none. It did not make sense to build on it when there were acres of derelict land in existing cities.

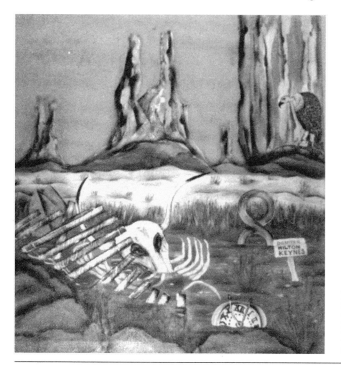

Poet and artist Bill Billings painted this nightmare vision of Milton Keynes during the early days.

Milton Keynes Development Corporation members, chief officers and advisors, 1967. They announced that the master plan would not be a once-and-for-all monolithic plan imposed on the residents of the area. Instead five local authorities, Wolverton, Bletchley, Newport Pagnell (Urban and Rural District Councils) and Winslow would be invited to join a liaison committee under the chairmanship of managing director W.N. Ismay.

Mrs A.M. Durbridge proudly displays her copy of the South East Planning Study, April 1967. A solicitor's wife, magistrate and mother, she thought that a woman's point of view could benefit the handling of the various social problems likely to arise when people moved into the city. She did not foresee any clash between her work as a county councillor and as a member of the Corporation.

There were many dreams and nightmares about Milton Keynes in the heady days of 1965. This is an artist's view of one dream: the proposed marina, with its imposing background of towering luxury flats. So that plans such as these could get under way, Mr W.N. Ismay was appointed full-time managing director of the Development Corporation, on £10,000 a year.

Lord 'Jock' Campbell of Eskan, photographed here in 1967, was the first Development Corporation chairman. His salary was £5,000 a year. There were already twenty-one new towns under construction when he started on Milton Keynes. The latter was expected to be among the biggest, with an intended population of around 250,000. The corporation planned for families with at least one car, a thirty hour working week and considerable leisure and shopping needs. Within weeks of his appointment Campbell revised the assessment of the city's building costs from £400 million to £500 million.

Maj. R.B. Verney, of the distinguished family famous for its support of Charles I during the Civil War. A county councillor and alderman, he was an obvious choice for Development Corporation membership. He was chairman of the Radcliffe Trust, the biggest landowner in the area (Dr John Radcliffe left a large sum to Oxford University in 1714 for medical establishments). Maj. Verney was also a former president of the County Landowners Association.

The Development Corporation gathered in the still remote and peaceful village of Milton Keynes. Here, before the Norman Conquest, Queen Edith had held the former manor. After the Conquest it passed to the De Catrines (or Keynes). The Corporation members are, from left to right, W.N. Ismay, A. Meikle, Lord Campbell, Lady Serota, H. Cutter, Mrs Durbridge, R. Verney and R. Bellchambers.

Ray Bellchambers reads an address at the opening of the first city road-construction works near Stony Stratford, 26 August 1970. Ray was chairman and veteran of Newport Pagnell Rural District Council. He embraced the new city project wholeheartedly, even though his lifelong Bradwell neighbourhood would be engulfed. This scene was shown on Anglia Television and by the next morning the Hymac digger had been stolen; a great amount of material and equipment was stolen from city building sites over the following years.

At the time of the South East Study (see p. 9) and Pooley plan (see p. 11) Sir Keith Joseph had been Housing and Local Government Minister. His Labour successor was Richard Crossman, photographed in 1964. New local Labour MP Bob Maxwell said he had been promised that his government would plan for the natural growth of Bletchley and the smaller towns: 'You can take it from me that the Pooley Plan for a monorail city of 250,000 will be well and truly dead.'

Mr Crossman had worked on wartime intelligence operations associated with Bletchley Park. He brought his considerable intelligence to the Battle of Bletchley and the wider South East Planning issues.

Politicians come and go, and Crossman went. However, Margaret Thatcher was around for what seemed to some a very long time. Here she is visiting Harold Wilson's brainchild, the Open University, on 10 January 1973. At this time she was Education Minister and known to some as 'Thatcher milk snatcher' because she cut the provision of free school milk.

She too had a mind for detail and radical ideas. The far right's choice for Tory Party leadership in 1975, she correctly gauged the country's mood in 1979 and so led a revolution in her people's outlook. Thus the city, conceived in a spirit of socialist planning idealism, gradually changed course. She is pictured in her memoirs, *The Downing Street Years*, proudly handing over deeds to one of the first tenants of the Milton Keynes Development Corporation, under the government's new right-to-buy scheme in September 1979.

Unfortunately this policy had the effect of raising house prices and thus shortening the housing supply to the less well off. Not surprisingly, in the first three days of 1995 Milton Keynes Borough Council received 31 applications from homeless people; 395 applications were made within three months over the summer, compared with 332 during the same period in 1994. (Open University)

Conceived in the spirit of Premier Harold Wilson's 'white hot technological revolution' speech of 1964, the Open University offered higher education to people in their living rooms, and thus brought hope to many. Here, it is about to go on air, in September 1981. BBC director general Alasdair Milne stands on the far right. He later resigned following conflict with Margaret Thatcher. (Open University)

Harold Wilson and his wife Mary visiting the Open University, 1982. A former Oxford don, Mr Wilson told David Frost that creating the Open University was the achievement he most wanted to be remembered for. Frost suggested renaming it to reflect the late premier's unique contribution. In 1995 the university has 143,173 registered students and 3,300 full-time staff. The local Dawson Road sorting office handles the mail which keeps the establishment in touch with students throughout the world. It has three sorting machines handling 30,000 letters an hour. (Open University)

Prince Charles's visit to the Open University, 14 May 1982. A Cambridge graduate with exacting ideas about architecture, one wonders what he made of the design of Milton Keynes. He certainly looks a little perplexed. It is doubtful that this would be his dream city. He did not visit Netherfield's housing development, though he might have noticed it as he passed because it is only a short distance west across Woughton Park. If he did, he might have agreed with Bill Billings, who mused: 'Netherfield, to lean and fade in such short time. Decay sighs in my step as I shop you 20 years on, no drowsy roots, grazing sheep. Sun-swept trees are not on this terrain.'

Bill was discovered by television writer Jack Story, while reading poetry at a Stantonbury Campus workshop. Working as a building-site lorry driver during the day, Bill was typecast as a Milton Keynes tipper-truck driver in the ATV drama documentary *Turn Back Dorothy*, a warning of the horrors that Milton Keynes would lead to. Nowadays he looks back on it all with black humour: 'Imagine them sitting there and deciding to build the crematorium between a place called Two Mile Ash and Kiln Farm. Milton Keynes is an illness, a symbol of Britain.'

Honoured by the Open University, Bill's zaniest adventure must have been when he painted a derelict New Bradwell pub three shades of pink in 1980: 'It was rat infested, popular with winos and one of the first things you saw as you left Wolverton station. At least my impromptu paintwork encouraged the brewery to demolish it.' (Open University)

Section Two

BARE BONES

One of construction firm Walter Llewellyn and Sons' earth-moving machines stands ready to prepare the ground at Windmill Hill for some of the first housing in the city, 1973.

Llewellyn's factory and staff at Bleak Hall, 1973. I remember working there at the time, making floor sections for Netherfield homes. I did that on one side of the factory floor. On the other side they made the roof and side frames. It was like a conveyor belt. There was a lot of noise and long shifts. The sections were taken by lorry to the sites for assembly and were clad in weatherproof materials. They went up much quicker than conventional buildings. These were boom days, and even though it was a brick-making area, bricks were scarce. Aluminium cladding was used instead for Netherfield.

In January 1968 Fred Pooley made known his dislike of this 'system' building in a lecture to the Royal Institute of British Architects in London: 'It would have been more in the nation's interest if a greater part of the intensive research of the last few years had gone into making traditional buildings with less concentration on system buildings which are now so prolific as to defeat their own subject.'

These views were of no concern to contractors or architects working on Netherfields. They simply had a job to do, ordained by higher powers. Netherfield homes were created by a team of designers known to their colleagues as 'the pop group' because of their early 1970s manner and style. The Netherfield plan was originally a design competition entry for a northern new town and was bought in by the Milton Keynes chief architect.

For Bill Barton, who became Llewellyn's contract manager, that meant getting his firm's Bleak Hall factory up and running. He travelled up from Eastbourne in November 1970 to look around.

Bill also had to get the first Llewellyn's building site at Windmill Hill under way. These are some of the ladies who supported him, along with his wife Barbara, during all the long hours of hard work. They are photographed at Bleak Hall in 1973.

Barbara said that Bill, inspired by the pioneering spirit with which the West was won, intended to conquer the wilds of north Bucks. No one he knew had heard of Windmill Hill, which he discovered was in Bletchley, not tiny Milton Keynes. It was an open field area next to a golf course, where plots of land were going at £4,000 a time, and he regrets to this day not snapping up a bundle.

Working night and day, Bill first lodged in Shenley Road Guest House and was on the lookout for a likely labour force. He remembers going into one pub while the main sewer work was in progress: 'It was full of Murphy's boys.' He recalls that his first employee was a delightful man named Mick, who took pride in making tea and keeping the company hut tidy. Then one day when he was walking along Bletchley's Queensway, at that time a noisy thoroughfare, he saw an advertisement for lodgings in Little Horwood, just outside the designated city area. There he discovered a prime mover among workers in Tony Whittingham. Llewellyn's never looked back.

Bill settled in Little Horwood and Barbara eventually joined him. She said: 'I think we were the first family up from Eastbourne. 'She told readers of the company newspaper in 1974: 'Milton Keynes is not a penal colony. Work brought us all here and it will bring many more families. Much as I regret the need for acres of good farming land to be swallowed up forever, I find the growth of the new city fascinating.'

Good footpaths and cycle ways were integral to city plans. Here a precast section is being lowered on to a new footbridge abutment at Tinker's Bridge, June 1975.

Meanwhile normal canal life rolls by unhindered on this bright summer day. The Grand Junction Canal, built between 1793 and 1800, connected London and the industrial Midlands. It changed much of the landscape. After the Second World War it became the Grand Union Canal. The waterway continues to be popular with leisure users. It has been well integrated as a feature of the city landscape. The towpaths make pleasant walks and cycleways.

Creating Milton Keynes was not just a matter of away with the old, on with the new. Many old buildings were lovingly restored with Development Corporation guidance and funding. Pete Sullivan is pictured here, in 1978, manhandling one of the four new load-bearing beams during the restoration of Bradwell Mill (see p. 100). Each new beam cost £1,000.

Purchased by the Corporation in 1969, the mill was a sorry sight when Pete walked past it with his fiancée in 1978. He uttered the immortal words: 'You know, it would be nice to get that mill running again.' He telephoned the Corporation the next day and so began fifteen months' hard labour. The mill had lost one sail in high winds and another had been removed for safety. New sails were made by the only millwright still working in England, Jim Davies of Lincolnshire. Most of the old timber was rotten. Pete said it was almost a rebuild instead of a patching-up job.

Birds (the feathered kind) were Pete's main company while he worked. 'They were a bit of a problem. They'd had the place to themselves for so long and made an awful mess.'

Pete observed that Bradwell was really a watermill area, and windmills were not very successful. Therefore £20,000 was well spent recreating something rare and of great educational value to visitors, residents and schoolchildren alike.

Milton Keynes Borough Council has provided for the mill's future by announcing its intention to establish the Friends of Bradwell, to act as a management team responsible for its day-to-day operation.

Bill Billings putting the finishing touches to his dinosaur creation at Pear Tree Bridge. He made sure that there was more to the new city than roads and roundabouts. Dinosaurs so fascinated him that he made a radio broadcast called *Death of a Dinosaur* and created Dinosaur Park with its display of bones. He is certainly a poet – some would say not a prophet, but prophets are rarely, if ever, welcome in their own land. This Bucks bard, whose family 'emigrated' to Islington, returned complete with cockney vowels, and is arguably much more potent than the usual Islington intellectual.

Stantonbury Campus from the air, 1977. Geoff Cooksey was the first director when it opened in 1974. The Labour government issued Circular Number 10 in 1965, requiring all counties to abolish grammar schools and develop comprehensives. The majority of Bucks resisted but Milton Keynes was virgin land and Stantonbury was designed to fit the new philosophy.

The school was still a building site when the first 230 students arrived. Nowadays it is the largest provider of secondary education in the county. One of the original staff, Roy Newitt, was recently honoured by the Open University for his role in Milton Keynes' arts. He founded the Stantonbury Campus Theatre Company and the Stantonbury Campus Youth Theatre. His other work includes collaborating with Roger Kitchen to establish the Living Archive project. This has led to plays and productions, based on taped memories, which are professionally produced and popular with all ages.

Looking back is sometimes controversial and inevitably selective. Not all of Milton Keynes is happy with its schools. Firebugs caused £1 million worth of damage in January 1988, just days after a mystery fire at Newport Pagnell's Ousedale School. More recently, in June 1995, vandals caused £1,000 worth of damage at Conniburrow Middle School.

In November 1994 Tory county councillors revived the idea of a Milton Keynes grammar school to separate a minority of academic pupils from the perceived distractions of an urban mix. Those who fail the selection test of the proposed new system could always opt into the city's well-established private sector. Renée Soskin started her preparatory school in 1970 when independent school fees were £35 a term. Demand led her to establish a senior school in Soskin Drive off Monks Way.

Technical staff at Marlborough Gate Bridge, city centre, April 1979. From left to right are Mr Bowles (bridge designer), Peter Clark (resident engineer), Brian O'Sullivan (clerk of the works), Andy Warren, Chas MacDonald and an unidentified student. Hard hats were just coming into 'fashion' and not a moment before time. I remember working in trenches over 17 ft deep at Woughton on the Green in 1971. My ganger, Cassidy, laughed when I asked for a helmet to protect me from lumps falling off the piles of 'muck' on either side of the trench. They were being shaken loose by the giant Euclid earth movers which were cutting out the road routes. Sometimes great lumps of clay would tumble down. But there was nothing more nerve-racking then watching little Paddy Brogan lower a 29 inch diameter concrete pipe down to us, using the boom of his Hymac digger as a crane. It was like the sword of Damocles, held in its sling only by a bar that was far too short. There wasn't even any shuttering up the sides of the trenches to stop them caving in.

Accidents did happen. Trenches did not have to be deep to be dangerous. Here Bletchley Fire Brigade has been called to the aid of a worker caught in a side collapse. This is the early 1970s and there is not a hard hat in sight.

This picture shows one of the main reasons for all the pipe laying. It is Cotton Valley sewage works, photographed by Ray Bellchambers from the Corporation helicopter, late 1970s. The filter beds are on the right. Back in 1966 Bletchley had been in turmoil over whether to use composting machinery to dispose of sewage. T. Dickens told a Council meeting: 'We shall have the biggest pile of muck in the kingdom and where shall we put it – in Queensway or the Council Chamber?'

Campbell Park, named after Corporation chairman Lord Campbell of Eskan. Lord Campbell died on Boxing Day 1994. In 1993 he said: 'I'm just glad I won't be around much longer to see Milton Keynes being wrecked.' Former Milton Keynes MP Bill Benyon hailed Lord Campbell, the borough's only freeman, as the architect of the new city. One wonders what the latter would have thought of plans to fell a hundred-year-old oak tree to make room for another shopping mall, on the opposite side of the main one in Midsummer Boulevard.

Brian O'Sullivan pressure-testing pipes near the building site of the central Milton Keynes police station, July 1983. The city's young trees are already doing well and are ready to complement the boulevard, which is seen here almost completed.

Getting business into Milton Keynes was seen as a major difficulty, and this persuaded the County Council to abandon its plan and back the government's New Town Development Corporation. With financial support from the Treasury, Milton Keynes was soon attracting enterprise. This modern office block is pictured during construction in October 1983. It became the headquarters of the Institute of Chartered Accountants.

The construction of Milton Keynes consumed a lot of concrete. Here the contractors Gallifords are building a footbridge over grid road H5, early 1980s.

Milton Keynes police station nearing completion, February 1984. Block paving is being laid down in the foreground; this gives a warmer appearance than the concrete paving slabs so common elsewhere in the city. Milton Keynes borough has a population of 176,330 (1991 census) and a lot of visitors. Crime and traffic problems are inevitable and varied. Statistically men are more likely to experience violent assault than women. Derek Dunkley was one such statistic. Two brutal muggers (one black, one white) attacked him in the city centre one Saturday night in 1994 as he went to buy prepayment electricity cards. Milton Keynes has also had its share of sex offences, murders, joy riding, bomb scares, vandalism and even a siege. Around eight hundred people from the borough go missing each year. Considering that the ultimate building blocks of so vast a settlement are its people, what else might we expect? The newcomers have helped to create a cosmopolitan area. There are great differences of age, experience and background here. Perhaps the most challenging differences are ethnic. In March 1993 the *Milton Keynes Gazette* reported: '[The city] is in the grips of a sickening bout of racism – and the culprits are the British National Party, it is claimed. . . . They have even handed out leaflets outside the schoolgates at Stantonbury. . . . Matters came to a head this weekend when a New Bradwell family huddled together in terror in their house as young thugs shouting racial abuse smashed seven windows with a hammer.'

Here Milton Keynes' development brought prosperity to local as well as larger contractors. Taylor's from Steeple Claydon are using their Akerman excavator on pipe works between the city centre and Foodhall, 1986. Clerk of the Works Brian O'Sullivan recalls that this machine was loading soil on to lorries opposite the police station in February 1987. This soil was taken to a site near the Peace Pagoda at Willen Lake, where he was watching it being tipped out: 'It was being used to create a mound for a footbridge. I noticed a piece of metal as it was poured on to the ground and thought it was strange because it was coming from virgin soil, off what had been a farm. I drove up to where they were digging it out and noticed a patch of oil. Digging around it, I found some other pieces with writing on that indicated it came from a crashed plane.' Brian then applied to the Ministry of Defence for a licence to dig deeper. This was granted, subject to a condition that he consult them should he find any ordnance or human remains. The bulk of the subsequent find was two Allison Aero engines (one with limited damage), three propeller blades, two superchargers and wing spar components. There were many smaller fragments. The Imperial War Museum at Duxford airfield identified the plane as a P38 Lightning. Chatting to local people, Brian discovered farm workers who remembered it crashing on Knotwood Field Farm in about 1943. The best propeller blade went to the local ATC and the remainder for possible display at Duxford. Building a new city thus provided an excellent opportunity for archaeology.

Brian O'Sullivan (left) joked that he was shark fishing in this photograph, June 1984. He was actually with assistant resident engineer Hamid Pourborzghi, helping to prepare the site for the city-centre Foodhall.

Formwork carpenters prepare the mould for concrete steps near the planned Foodhall site, November 1984. The indent in the concrete wall was left to house discreet lighting, so crucial to safety in the underpasses.

The roof is put on a city-centre underpass near the Foodhall, 1984.

There are plenty of opportunities for people to take a step up in Milton Keynes, even if it is only on the hundreds of concrete ones dotted around the city centre. Here workmen are putting the finishing touches to a set of steps near the Foodhall in 1984.

Looking north towards the city-centre shops, November 1984. The road under construction on the right was to lead to the Foodhall.

Neathill housing development, August 1985. This was originally intended as cheap, self-build housing plots, but the boom years encouraged speculative builders into the area and prices rose.

Milton Keynes paving slabs at their best, March 1985. The skeleton of the radically new Point cinema is rising in the background. Brian O'Sullivan said: 'It seemed strange to see them building a multi-screen cinema at a time when home videos were keeping people at home. But it seems to have worked.' Sadly, smaller cinemas in neighbouring Bletchley and Buckingham did feel the effects and closed down.

Outside the Foodhall, March 1985. Customers were already coming from far and wide to shop at Milton Keynes. The Foodhall was a sound enterprise because there was bound to be a crowd for cut-price food. Here the road is being prepared with 'black top' in readiness for the influx. Further plans to extend the shopping area have caused controversy. The first came following the animal rights attack on Dickins and Jones in January 1989. Fire caused £10 million worth of damage. Redevelopment brought a large Marks and Spencer store, which extended across a public square. Development Corporation pioneer Ray Bellchambers criticized this, because he felt that the square should have remained a space for public assembly and peaceful protest.

A bore hole is being made to assess ground conditions, before foundations can be designed for a footbridge over the canal near the Japanese School (route H5).

Looking south-west across the Grand Union Canal towards the Japanese School, 1986. The 'false works' are in place ready for the construction of the H5 bridge over the canal. A pleasure boat sets off this sunny scene.

A closer view of the canal bridge works, 1986. A geological fault on the east side necessitated digging foundations 63 ft deep. The 'safety boat' on the canal was required in case any one fell into the water.

Here concrete is being poured into the canal bridge works. In the background is the Japanese School.

Building energy-efficient housing at Shenley Lodge, February 1987. These properties are on the western fringe of the city and are imaginative in design.

Mike Eastham was running his own consultancy in energy-efficient heating systems for industry and schools when he moved his family up to Shenley Lodge from Sussex. Naturally he appreciated the benefits of this energy-efficient property, which he and his wife (seen here peeping through the incomplete garage window) decided to buy in 1987. Mrs Elizabeth Eastham said she could not think of a better place to live and bring up a family than Milton Keynes: 'It combines the best of city and rural life. There is so much going on in Milton Keynes,' she said.

Bridge works near Caldicot Lake, early 1980s. The Abundance Garden Centre, on the right, prospered when all this open country was quickly filled up with housing.

The construction of the aqueduct to take the canal over Grafton Street, 1987.

With so much concrete going into the new city, it would not do to get the mixture wrong. These men are working for Mentors at Kiln Farm and they are conducting 'slump tests' on the concrete to make sure it is strong enough.

Graham Pateman takes a breather at bridge works over route V11, near the Walnut Tree pub. Gallifords were the main contractors; they poured as much as 35,000 cu. ft of concrete in one day.

At the same bridge works these men are checking the concrete mixture just before pouring it, to ensure that it is the correct consistency. A specialist firm called Pochins supplied the pumping equipment.

The concrete can now be pumped – and here it goes.

Energy-efficient housing at Shenley, photographed by Mike Eastham at the time of the Energy World Exhibition, 1988. The wind generator, visible in the top left of the picture, is no longer in use, because it was considered too noisy by some residents. Margaret Thatcher visited this exhibition and was full of praise for its achievements. Walter Llewellyn and Sons at Milton Keynes were major house builders in the city and they designed a house for the exhibition. It was inspected by the National Energy Foundation, which gave it a National Home Energy Rating (NHER) of ten-plus on a scale of nought to ten. Remarkably it could be heated for £30 a year. Analysis also demonstrated that a standard Llewellyn timber-frame house with a floor area of 1,000 sq. ft could give a fuel saving of more than £100 per annum over a new house built to current building regulations.

The city has been growing since 1970. Here, near Furzton Lake, Shenley, it takes a little winter sleep, December 1985.

Wide awake again, the city keeps on growing. Here we see an aqueduct being built to carry the canal over the extension to Grafton Street, 1991. (Rose Callow)

The Church of Christ the Cornerstone nearing completion, 1990. It is viewed from what was a city square until the Marks and Spencer extension encroached on it in 1994. Though this church looks like a mini St Paul's, it is no more a cathedral than Milton Keynes is officially a city. Its priest, Father Bennie Noonan, celebrated twenty-five years in the priesthood in June 1995, and his 86-year-old mother made her second trip out of Ireland to enjoy his celebrations at Coffee Hall. Father Noonan said that he finds his work at Milton Keynes very exciting because it brings him into contact with five major Christian denominations.

NAKED CITY
IMAGES

An interesting image hanging over the MADCAP

arts centre doorway, Wolverton. Is the city just as

'madcap'?

The Eastham children playing on the concrete cows at Bradwell, 1991. These cows have become synonymous with Milton Keynes, yet they were just an art project and were not meant to be a permanent statement. Train riders look out for them and make jokes. Others are not so amused by any of the city sights. The late playwright John Osborne observed: 'Every time I travel to London by train I pass through this deranged planners' Utopia and look away. Nothing is more depressing, not even the industrial wastes of Sandwell and Dudley, than this gleaming gum boil plonked in the middle of England. Even the saplings, planted half-heartedly by the station, never seem to make it.'

Milton Keynes Borough Council decided to fight such criticism by announcing a Festival of Humour for 1995, believing that it would attract tourism. Mayor Edward Ellis said his favourite joke is: 'Why is Milton Keynes the fairground of Britain? Because it has so many roundabouts.'

The precision of the grid road system is well displayed in this view of Central Milton Keynes Shopping Centre at the Middle Bridge section, late 1970s. London Brick Landfill won the contract to handle waste from the 180 tenants, ranging from John Lewis to the smallest confectioner.

The old LNWR station at Bletchley was the makeshift station for the city until this modern masterpiece opened in 1982. Standing in the old parish of Loughton, it handles two hundred trains a day. The station is still very much on the edge of the city.

Milton Keynesian Chris Wright has been a driving force behind the attempt by the Oxford and Bucks Rail Action Committee to get the Milton Keynes to Oxford section of the old 'Varsity' railway line reopened. This picture shows the committee's first 'Christmas shopper' train from Aylesbury to Milton Keynes at Winslow, November 1984.

Steve Hawkes, British Rail area manager, aboard the shopper train. Sadly, when Amey Roadstone stopped running its gravel trains from Wolverton in 1990, the line was mothballed and hopes for a new service faded. (There is talk of making it a long-distance cycle way.) Strangely Labour's Barbara Castle closed the line to passengers against Beeching's advice in 1967 – at the very moment the new city was planned.

The railway viaduct from Haversham, 1991. Dealing with surface water was a major obstacle for city planners. The flood level of the River Ouse in this picture indicates the problem. A small German plane crashed near the viaduct during the Second World War. Baden Powell of the Home Guard said: 'We'd see these little German planes going over on reconnaissance. We never took much notice.' German prisoners-of-war worked on the land or in local brickworks.

The establishment of the open market in Milton Keynes city centre in 1979 drew a lot of business away from Bletchley market. Here, in 1994, the bus on the bridge carries an advertisement for Aylesbury's rival centre. Being only 18 miles away, Aylesbury felt the effects of Milton Keynes' success, and pursued rigorous redevelopment in a bid to recapture shoppers.

The queen first visited Milton Keynes in June 1979 to open the shopping centre. Here she is pictured on a return visit for the official opening of De Montfort University, 13 March 1992. This was formerly The Polytechnic, Milton Keynes. De Montfort has the advantage of being located in pleasant rural surroundings and also being at the hub of a modern business centre. The Development Corporation invited tenders from established universities and polytechnics to develop a new higher-education campus; they wanted a complete range of educational facilities in the Milton Keynes conurbation. Leicester Polytechnic (which was soon to become De Montfort) won, and work began in 1990. One of the students at the opening ceremony said: 'Afterwards people kept saying, "Yes, she [the queen] spoke to me. They were so excited. After she was gone, the atmosphere was electric. Everybody wanted to talk about it."'

When the queen's infamous daughter-in-law Sarah Ferguson visited in the early 1990s there was a similarly large crowd.

Preparing a poster for something else 'madcap'. This was for the 1987 production of *The Matchgirls* at the St George's Institute, Wolverton. MADCAP in this case stands for Music And Drama Community Arts Project.

A scene from *The Matchgirls* at St George's Institute. The institute was built in 1908 with railway company money and was designed to serve the leisure and educational needs of local people. The MADCAP Trust bought the derelict institute in 1981, and planned to transform it into a youth arts base. The Development Corporation gave financial assistance. Drama, music and writing groups began working here in 1987.

Building Central Milton Keynes railway station, July 1981. Nowadays over three thousand people commute to London daily and many more commute to Milton Keynes. The London link is so strong that in 1995 there was an outcry at the prospect of an end to broadcasts by London's Carlton TV. (Colin Stacey)

The railway station concourse presents an attractive scene in modern terms, and is very popular with skate boarders. The replica Bloomer engine, on the left, was built by Wolverton apprentices. The original was designed by the loco superintendent at Wolverton, J.E. McConnell; it replaced the ineffective four-wheeled Bury engines in the early 1850s.

Putting the finishing touches to Neath Hill, early 1980s. Fred Diper, left, was the foreman for P.J. Carey – a significant contributor to the building of the city.

Bill Billings fast asleep inside his Pear Tree Bridge dinosaur. He didn't have planning permission to build it and this was the only way he could stop the 'authorities' pulling it down. Luckily they saw sense, and this major statement about the new city remains.

Here are some of the children who worked with Bill Billings on community arts projects in the mid-1970s. On 9 April 1988 *The Independent* wrote of Bill: 'He is as much a clown, a cartoonist and conjuror. He appears on Buckinghamshire Television [a local cable company] children's programmes demonstrating how to make weird and wonderful objects out of junk.'

Bill Billings' upside-down suit dominates this crazy parade through the underpasses, mid-1970s.

The opening of Stantonbury Campus sports hall, mid-1970s. The boy at the front right looks better equipped for windsurfing than table tennis! (Stantonbury Campus)

Hilary Davan Wetton conducting the Milton Keynes Chamber Orchestra in February 1975. The leader is Diana Cummings. Creating and maintaining a professional orchestra required enormous effort. The orchestra's base moved to the idyllic surroundings of the Rosebery Rooms at Woolstone in the 1980s, then to Midsummer Boulevard in 1994. Ken Chaproniere took over as general manager in 1991 and has attracted generous support from many local and international companies.

It had all started at Stantonbury Theatre, when Hilary Davan Wetton had stood on the stage and said: 'This is an ideal theatre for small-scale concerts.' With no professional orchestra in the area, Milton Keynes had a cultural gap to fill.

Newport Pagnell and Olney Lions Club organized an event to mark the launch of the Willen Hospice extension appeal, in December 1992. The Britannia Chamber Orchestra gave a performance. Derek Nimmo, famous for his role as the Revd Mervyn Noote in the 1966 television comedy *All Gas and Gaiters*, is seated second from the right. Sir John Reid is seated second from the left.

Willen photographed from the air, late 1980s. The edge of the artificial lake is visible in the bottom corner. Like Furzton Lake, it was constructed to facilitate drainage and to add a feature to the area. However, there is some concern over algae and pollution.

The manor of Willen was bought by Dr Richard Busby in 1672. As headmaster of Westminster School for more than half of the seventeenth century, it was said that he birched knowledge into the youth of England. He might become a model for future teachers! Many of his pupils achieved great success, including John Dryden and John Locke; at one time sixteen of his old boys were bishops. One grateful old pupil, scientist Robert Hooke, provided him with designs for Willen's most peculiar church (top centre of the picture). This was built in 1679 at a cost of £5,000, using material from the previous church. The old manor-house was rebuilt early in the nineteenth century. It was extended in the 1980s, by which time it had become Willen Hospice. As such it had an ideal setting, near the calm water and in sight of the Peace Pagoda.

A hospice was originally a refuge for early Christian pilgrims. Such a shelter would have been run by a religious order, with staff also looking after the poor, sick and dying. When Henry VIII broke with the Roman Catholic Church most hospices closed. The Hospice of St John, near Willen, was typical; it served pilgrims travelling to Norfolk. The name of the modern hospice here incorporates the old name with the image of Mary tending Jesus on the cross; hence it is called the Hospice of Our Lady and St John. The hospice is non-denominational, offering care to the terminally ill throughout the area. It is an independent charity, and relies heavily on financial support from the community that it serves. (Commission for New Towns)

Reg Perkins and his wife Nellie stand beside Val Cassidy, matron of Willen Hospice, November 1984. Reg is proudly displaying his watercolour of the original manor-house at Willen. The picture continues to sell in print form, thus providing much-needed funds for the hospice. Voluntary worker Dorothy Francis is on the far right, holding another of Reg's works. Reg was a member of a local art society and illustrated Jim Styles' book on the area called *From Romans to Roundabouts*.

Princess Diana gives her famous coy smile to the camera as she leaves Willen Hospice after her visit, in April 1986.

A growing city means lots of babies. Mothercare is just ahead of these advancing pushchairs, April 1985.

Dorothy Murley, aged nearly eighty, heads home to native Cornwall, via Milton Keynes bus station, April 1985. When she arrived for a holiday she told relatives: 'I wish I'd gone to Scotland.' But when she saw the shopping centre she could not stop singing its praises: 'They've got nothing like it in Cornwall.'

The Peace Pagoda by Willen Lake was the idea of architect Tom Hancock, who, Ray Bellchambers recalls, was Buddhist by inclination. Don Ritson was the Corporation architect. The ceremony to lay the foundation stone was held on 8 April 1979, close to the old church. A newspaper commented: 'It will be to some disturbing, to others inspiring, to see the church and the pagoda sitting so close together. The sight could hardly fail to make one stop and think. Perhaps about peace, perhaps not.'

The girls in this picture are from Newport Pagnell, on the city fringe, where 'there's nothing to do', and the boys are from Fishermead. They were photographed in May 1995. They are very different from the youths on pages 12 and 13. These teenagers inhabit a world of high unemployment, crime, homelessness and pressures to consume. Central Milton Keynes is a mecca for consumers, who come from many miles beyond the city limits.

The Point, central Milton Keynes, was opened by AMC in June 1985. It is now owned by UCI. The latter shelved plans to double the number of screens to ten. Even so The Point is credited with reviving the fortunes of the British cinema. Steve Knibbs, UK managing director of UCI cinemas, explained: 'People said it wouldn't work. The ticket price started at £1.95. We based it on the cost of two pints of bitter. Pricing was very important because people had got out of the habit of going to the cinema.' (Thames Valley Police)

A concert at the National Bowl, Milton Keynes, late 1980s. Rock and roll is a tribal thing. Home-grown news photographer Peter Orme remembers his heady days photographing stars such as Freddie Mercury and David Bowie. Peter began as an amateur in 1979, using a girlfriend's camera. He said: 'Geoff Ross of the *Milton Keynes Mirror* encouraged me to become professional in 1981. The local news-gathering has changed a lot since then. The sport was good. I enjoyed covering Luton Town FC. It's a shame they didn't move to Milton Keynes after all. Rhythmic gymnastics at Bletchley Leisure Centre was also good fun and speedway at the Groveway. When we got the World Power Lifting Championships and the Bowl concerts you knew Milton Keynes was on the map.'

Award-winner Peter now works for the *Daily Telegraph*. It is a far cry from his first job, with the local *Citizen* paper, for which he developed pictures in his bedroom at Conniburrow. 'Other local papers didn't take us seriously. I think that's why we succeeded.' The *Citizen* is now part of the EMAP group, where award-winning photographers such as Charlie Wooding maintain the high standard. (Thames Valley Police)

C-shift, Wolverton police station, 1982. From left to right: Mick Adams, Dave Giles, Mick Clanfield, Tony Burton, Steve Roebuck. (Thames Valley Police)

Steve Roebuck on patrol at Wolverton station, 1982. This is very much a Z Cars image. It is a pity that it's too dark to see the even more historical railway station. This wooden building, dating from 1881, stood on brick arches over the tracks. It was demolished in 1991 to make way for something more cost effective. (Thames Valley Police)

Woodhill Prison. This was built in response to a 1984 Home Office review called *Managing the Long Term Prison System*. The design was also influenced by US research. Work was completed quickly, between 1988 and 1991, to relieve pressure on other prisons. The complex was screened by trees and earth mounds. Dedicated managers look after groups of prisoners; Julie Cooney was nominated for a local Employee of the Year award for her smile and for her caring approach to inmates' problems in a volatile place – so volatile that in 1995 one prisoner held a woman officer at knife point for twenty-nine hours.

Opening day celebrations at Milton Keynes Marina, near Woughton on the Green, 1988. Work started on the project in 1986. Peter Sullivan had been subcontracting for the firm building the marina. The original company which wanted the marina to be built pulled out, and Peter became the owner of the partly built marina. When it was finished he set up a management company to run it. There is space for 110 boats, and with the boom in leisure traffic Peter's company has no trouble filling it.

Milton Keynes Marina, photographed from the air, 1988. It is interesting to contrast this with the artist's impression produced in the 1960s (see p. 18). (Peter Sullivan)

Futuristic housing set beside the canal at Pennylands, Milton Keynes. The city embraces a variety of architectural styles.

John Cox hung up his running spikes in the late 1970s and followed a local tradition inspired by Bletchley cycle hero 'Goz' Goodman in the 1960s. John is seen here riding for the A5 Rangers in a 10 mile open race along the A5(D), 1984.

Maggie Philbin and the *Tomorrow's World* crew visit Milton Keynes, 1988 – where else could they be with those concrete cows in the background? The crew had come to try out inventor Pete Sullivan's patent triangular wheel. Pete developed the caterpillar device for his pile-driving vehicles, which work close to soggy waterside building sites. This reinvention of the wheel spreads the load over a greater area and reduces the chance of sinking in. Pete, primarily an engineer, is a man of energy, imagination and character. He has built local playground facilities and so much more (see pp. 28 and 71). He has clearly been inspired by the opportunities created by life in Milton Keynes.

Local police extras on the set of *Indiana Jones and the Temple of Doom*, which was filmed in the area during the 1980s. From left to right: Jeff Parker, Bob Brill, Gerry Freeman, Frank Grover. Milton Keynes city centre was used as a location for *Superman*, starring Christopher Reeve.

The Duchess of Gloucester opening Hazard Alley, November 1993. The alley was the brainchild of crime prevention officer PC Alan Brooks, on the right. His idea was inspired by the number of schoolchildren visiting his safety exhibition for schools. He went to the boardrooms of major companies to get financial backing. Hazard Alley was established in a Milton Keynes warehouse, and has lifelike sets of a house, garden, building site, garage forecourt, playground, farmyard and a railway. (Thames Valley Police)

Volkswagen GB's 23 acre central warehouse and headquarters at Blakelands, east Milton Keynes. Blakelands roundabout is at the top of the picture. The edge of Tongwell Lake is just visible at the bottom left; less than a mile below that is the M1 motorway.

Volkswagen was one of the first companies to show confidence in Milton Keynes as a business centre. The move to Blakelands resulted in the closure of five of its regional parts warehouses and its headquarters at Purley, Surrey. The project was first mooted in 1973, when the cost of investment would have been £4.5 million. A fuel crisis and falling car sales delayed the decision until February 1977, by which time the cost had risen to £7.5 million. The move enabled long-term cost cutting and a better service to customers. Volkswagen had resisted government pressure to go to development areas such as Runcorn or London's Docklands. Such sites did not meet the company's requirements for a place in the centre of the country and close to motorways. Every effort was made to move existing Volkswagen workers to Milton Keynes. (Volkswagen AG)

The Concrete Cowboys, 1993. From left to right: Mike Carne, Andy Powell, John Farthing. A lot of music is made in Milton Keynes – so much that Chappell of Bond Street opened a shop in the city centre.

The Concrete Cowboys met at a party. Andy said: 'We discovered a similar weird taste in music. We've played some superb venues such as the Stables at Wavendon, the North Wales Bluegrass Festival and most pubs in Milton Keynes. There have been memorable moments, including the drunk cleaning ladies who tried to snatch the microphones off us to sing Kenny Rogers' 'Lucille'. The Cowboys do a good version of Dylan's 'You ain't goin' nowhere', which might be something of a statement on the city's future now that the Commission for New Towns is so close to being wound up.

Section Four

THE WAY THEY
WERE

A quiet scene near Haversham's Norman church, close to the Northants county boundary,

1930s.

The view from Bow Brickhill, late 1940s. The woodland rises up to 600 ft and is home to a country club. It is part of the Duke of Bedford's estate, and lies about 3 miles south-east of Bletchley. Nowadays this outlook is filled by the new city, whose many lights twinkle at night-time.

Bradwell. The writer J.H. Peel noted in 1949 that this place, 'with half a hundred other hamlets, waits patiently for what the times will bring; not greatly changed since Drake sent his fire ships into Calais'. But it is easy to romanticize the 'old days'. The reality could be somewhat harsher. In January 1897 Bradwell Parish Council heard a complaint about an open sewer between High Street and School Street, New Bradwell.

New Bradwell. In 1856 the London & North Western Railway decided to expand its railway works for locomotive building. Lots of workers' terraced houses surrounding the site had to go. The railway company owned 15 acres of farmland between the canal and Newport turnpike. There they built the new housing, complete with pub, and this area was called New Bradwell.

London Road, Loughton. The London to Holyhead telegraph poles date this picture to around the turn of the century. Villagers were alarmed to hear Fred Pooley tell a Parish Council meeting in February 1965 that he wanted their village for his city centre. There was concern as to how elderly people would adjust to a new life in flats.

Here two of the genteel Field family members enjoy the Old Rectory gardens at Milton Keynes. The eighteenth-century building was home to generations of clergy, who had been chosen by the local aristocracy.

Their Lordships also held sway over this Milton Keynes village inn, The Old Swan, which was part of the manor's estate. In the 1890s the landlord, F. Barker, took delivery of Hipwell's beer from Olney twice each year. Thinking it too strong, he would allow drinkers only 2 pints a day, at 4*d* a pint. John Rose succeeded Arthur Bird as landlord in 1940. When new city proposals were published in 1965 he feared that his pub, with its old oak beams, high-back benches and chattering locals, would be no more. He also feared for the 700-year-old St Mary's Church where he had been organist since 1912. Both the church and the Old Swan, Phipps brewery's oldest pub, were conserved.

The water pump at Emberton (north of the new city), early 1900s. Disease could spread because of unclean water, and improvements were resisted owing to the cost to ratepayers. Scarlet fever, typhoid and diphtheria were particular nuisances at this time. The guardians paid £63 for tents to be erected in Little Woolstone Lane for a smallpox hospital. The guardians were local worthies chosen under the terms of the 1834 Poor Law Amendment Act to look after the poor, and related matters.

Council housing in Newport Pagnell. The Rural District Council began its scheme to build better homes for working people in the 1930s. Those pictured are rather different from the high-density, system-build units in some parts of the new city. Nevertheless, the latter did much to improve the quality of housing for many newcomers. Nowadays right-to-buy schemes have reduced the supply of low-cost housing.

Sheep-dipping at Emerson Farm, Shenley Brook End, early 1920s. The village and this way of working are long gone. Solicitor James Marchant appealed to fellow residents to fight development plans for Loughton and the Shenleys in 1967. He said: 'I am surprised by the defeatism which seems to have descended on everybody.'

The Methodist chapel is the centrepiece of this view of Simpson, 1908. Baden Powell, who came to the village in 1938, recalls: 'From the Woughton side you looked down on the village and saw a sea of blossom in the spring. There's practically nothing left of that now. It used to be a proper village. Everybody looked after everybody else. When they built the bus shelter it was an ideal spot to sit on a sunny day. We had all we needed here. Bakers, grocers and "packmen" called with things to sell us. They were the social workers. They took messages and helped you out.'

Simpson post office, 1912. Baden Powell has lived here since the 1940s and remembers the bypass that never came. Even so, the village was jammed up with traffic when the city building started: 'The road was 3–4 inches deep in mud from the lorries carrying away the muck from earthworks up in Woughton. It sprayed all up our windows.'

Simpson village in the late nineteenth century. There was big upheaval in the early 1970s when contractors encamped here to work in nearby Woughton on the Green, an ancient village, which was virtually destroyed by development. A Simpson villager recalls his wife's response when asked by a lorry driver if she knew where he could find Amey Roadstone (a building aggregate supplier). She replied innocently, 'I have never heard of her. She doesn't live around here.'

Simpson village hall (left), 1920s. It was an old wooden First World War hut, brought up from the transit camp at Fenny Stratford, between the A5 and the canal. North Bucks MP Robert Maxwell used to hold election meetings here during the early 1960s.

Floodwater in Simpson village, winter 1954. The cyclist seems to be only a little daunted by the problem. Today's Milton Keynes has better drainage and a network of Redway paths for cyclists and pedestrians.

Newport Road, Stantonbury. The original village has virtually disappeared, having been largely swallowed up by the new Stantonbury built nearby.

Carr's Mill, Stantonbury Low. This looks like an excellent place to stand and stare on a dreamy summer's day. Work in the fields may have been long and hard, work at school and on the railway could not have been easy, but at least folk could keep in touch with nature, and other species had a chance back in the 1930s.

The Barge Inn at Little Woolstone, 1880s. It served food and ale to passing bargees on the Grand Junction Canal, and it fared better than a good many other pubs when the railways came. In Stony Stratford the number of stage-coaches each week fell from 280 in 1835 to 12 in 1844. Farriers, wheelwrights and blacksmiths suffered too.

Old Wolverton Mill. In the 1890s Mr Woods, the miller, and his family suffered during a typhoid epidemic. The Ouse was a sluggish and polluted river, and the task of improving it was a brain teaser.

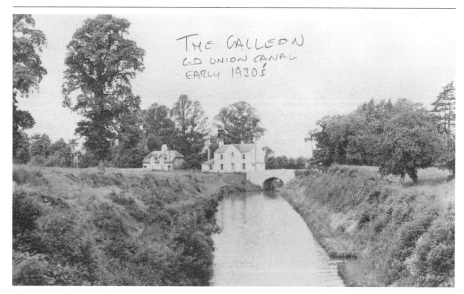

Clement Shorter observed in his *Highways and Byways* that 'Wolverton is an ugly centre of the railway industry . . . some 5,000 men being employed [in 1910].' He added: 'There are two Wolvertons – old and new.' This scene shows the old: the Galleon pub by the Grand Union Canal in the early 1930s.

The recreation ground, off Victoria Street, Wolverton. It was built in the 1930s and was the venue for Boy Scouts' bonfire night revels.

The swimming pool at Wolverton. This was built with donations given to mark Queen Elizabeth's coronation in 1953. Built close to Radcliffe School and the site of the present College of Further Education, it became very popular.

Stratford Road, Old Wolverton, late 1920s. McCorquodale's print works dominate the view. An important local employer, the family lived at Winslow Hall, with its large estate, and they were popular with royalty. The old works premises have been replaced by modern ones on the opposite side of the road, but business still thrives – the company now produces a lot of plastic credit cards. Such prosperity does not benefit many smaller firms. Dorothy Cox remembers a thriving market, which was held in the old school, with lovely flower stalls: 'It was a day out to visit. We used to meet the men there. So much has gone since the new city came. We used to have a Co-op with a drapery and furniture department – all gone.'

The Empire cinema, Wolverton, 1937. This had replaced the original cinema, but it suffered in the post-war decline. When the rival Palace closed in February 1961, the Empire seized its opportunity, purchasing 170 reconditioned seats and improved sound equipment. But owner London and Provincial Cinemas was unable to make a profit and closed it in 1969. The building was bought by the General Post Office and became a sorting-office extension.

THE PALACE, WOLVERTON

TOMORROW, SATURDAY

DANCING

TO BRYAN AND THE BRUNELLS
AND SUPPORTING GROUPS
8 p.m. to 11.45 p.m. Admission 5/-

COMING SOON
"THE TRUTH"

BINGO!

EVERY FRIDAY, SUNDAY, AND WEDNESDAY.
DOORS OPEN 7 p.m.
COMMENCING 8 p.m.
Finish 9 p.m. sharp

20 cash prizes

join now

NEW MEMBERS WELCOME

MONDAY

POP DANCING

TO POPULAR GROUPS
8 p.m. to 10.30 p.m. Admission 2/6

The Palace struggled on through the 1960s as a centre for new fashions in pop music, dancing and, above all, bingo, as this poster from February 1966 indicates. The owner, Mr Moss, retired to Winslow.

This fire at Whaddon Hall broke out during the conversion into a country hotel, early 1970s. The hall, former home of Baron de Wilton and later antiquarian Browne Willis, had been completely destroyed by fire in the late eighteenth century. No fireman could easily approach Whaddon in those days. In 1810 Revd St John Priest noted: 'The byroads of Bucks are extremely bad . . . the difficulty of finding the way from Fenny Stratford to Whaddon was such that without a guide I could not have surmounted it.'

Stacey Avenue, Wolverton, 1930s. This was a far cry from the town's earlier terraces. Land was relatively cheap at the time, so the gardens were generous. The area had a foretaste of trees in the streets – for which Milton Keynes is now famous.

St George's Way, Wolverton. The 1960s tower block on the right stood for modern living and was very much an ideal of the time. This used to be a different world. The railway works superintendent's house stood here, complete with a gardener's lodge at the gates. The superintendent reigned over an engineer, four overlookers and nine foremen in 1851. Gwen Brocklehurst, whose family came from Scotland to work at Wolverton, remembers her eldest sister working as a parlour maid for the superintendent in the 1930s. 'You'll do ever so well with good pay and independence, Katherine,' her grandmother said, encouraging her to take the job.

The River Ouse at Olney, late 1940s. Olney was the first local town to receive a plan for its future in relation to Milton Keynes. The river was to be cleaned by getting the tannery to allow trade wastes into public sewers via the tannery, homes were to be improved, unfit properties cleared and a small industrial estate established.

Mrs Isobel lived at Old Farm, Loughton, where there was still no electricity, gas or road in 1966. Her pony and cart were better suited than a motor vehicle to the terrain in wet weather. All was a far cry from the city tarmac and pretty lights that were on their way. She said: 'Of course it will mean we shall have to go, but my biggest regret will be the good hunting ground that will be lost.'

Real cows languishing in the fields around Great Linford, late 1940s.

Castlethorpe School, 1904. At this time the County Council had just taken control and established a coordinated system for the twentieth century. Education was still very much a matter of the three Rs and firm discipline.

John Cox snr ready for a game of football in Bradwell Church School playground, 1920s. In those days professional players earned no more than a craftsman in Wolverton works. John gave this picture to his sweetheart Dorothy when they were pupils together. Dorothy remembers her first day, sitting on the hall floor: 'Mum left me. I said, could I go to the toilet. I ran across the playground to Back Way and School Street. I was running down there shouting "Mum, mum". My mum was in a friend's house who had just had a baby. She said, "That's our Dorothy." I said, "It's me alright."'

Wolverton Grammar Street, Moon Street, early 1920s. The headmaster at this time was Mr Morgan. Poorer children fought for the few free places, and gained great status if successful. Academic standards were high. All ended when Milton Keynes established comprehensives and the new Radcliffe School opened in Aylesbury Street.

Girls' School, Wolverton, early 1900s. The infant classes were mixed. The upper school's girls' entrance was at the rear. Gwen Brocklehurst remembers her teacher, Miss Townsend, being 'firm but thorough. She was treated with respect. Her successor, Dorothy Starmmer Smith didn't believe in formal lessons. She formed a girls' choir and put on Shakespeare plays. I was a little fairy in *A Midsummer Night's Dream*.'

Science and Art Institute, Wolverton, 1920s. This was built by the railway, with financial assistance from institutions such as City and Guilds. Gwen Brocklehurst's grandfather was one of the main engravers of a large plaque in the hallway of the building, which depicted all the institutions which had provided money. There was an excellent technical school within, offering day and night classes for self-improvement. Girls were encouraged to do commercial subjects. The building was burnt out and became unsafe in the 1960s.

Bletchley and District Co-operative Society started in 1884 when railway workers clubbed together to buy essential goods at wholesale prices. This picture shows their first department store in Albert Street, 1901.

The Wolverton and Stony Stratford Tramways Company was formed in November 1882. Strangely, this local company bought engines from German archrivals to power its first double-decker tramcars (shown here). Each car carried 120 workmen to Wolverton railway works. Takings soon topped £45 a week and the daily fare of 1s ate into the men's weekly wage of 25s. But with boots at 7s a pair, it was almost cheaper than walking. There was no tramline from Wolverton to Newport Pagnell in 1899. Dorothy Hughes, born in Windsor Street, remembers her father having to walk this distance to fetch a doctor.

The restrictions of rails were soon abandoned for speedier motor buses. Fast travel has its dangers, as can be seen here. Bletchley Fire Brigade attended this burnt-out school bus on the M1 in 1959.

Wolverton railway works smithing shop, *c.* 1910. Jack Cox recalls his works days with pride: 'As a boy I remember taking dinners up to the men from Bradwell during my school dinner hour. I had a little truck with pram wheels on it. The men used to have a mess room. They'd eat up there and brew tea. I followed in my father John's footsteps. He was a saw sharpener. We built and housed the royal train. Whenever it went out a man from every trade went with it. Royal trains used to be painted with gold leaf. The Coronation Scot coaches were all built here. We used a lot of timber on the coaches and wagons. Two tons fell on my father once. But we didn't have many accidents. It was a hard life, but we were happy. Men were sometimes carried out overcome by heat from the moulding shop and we had some big fires. During the war "Lord Haw Haw" [William Joyce, an Irish propagandist for Nazi Germany] said: "You needn't bother camouflaging Wolverton works – we know it's there."' The closest bombs fell on Bradwell, killing five.

Threshing the corn, as shown here in fields near Loughton, was a laborious task. It was made a little easier by the use of a steam engine for the threshing box. E.H. Roberts of nearby Deenshanger iron works was a main supplier of efficient farm implements at this time.

A traction engine towing two large tree trunks to saw mills at Fenny Stratford, *c.* 1905.

Stoke Goldington's steam roller, early 1900s. Newport Pagnell Rural District Council took office in 1895, with responsibility for most of the highways southwards as far as Bletchley. Shenley parish's request for a steam roller was refused and the cost of highway maintenance was a worry. The County Council did not take control until 1931, and before then standards varied. In 1896 Councillor R. Wylie suggested a return to old methods with 'a capable ratepayer to oversee its own roads other than the main roads'. This was refused and the Rural District Council appointed W.H. Smith as highway surveyor. The Council bought 4,740 tons of granite chippings for £1,770 to improve road surfaces.

'Nobby Newport' was the locals' affectionate name for this little train seen here approaching Bradwell station, 1950. It carried workmen from Newport Pagnell to Wolverton railway works. The last service ran on 5 September 1964. The mill in the background was built in 1815 by Samuel Holman, using local limestone. It had been disused for some years when this picture was taken. (B. Brooksbank)

By the completion of the London–Birmingham railway in 1838 many physical obstacles had been overcome and lives lost. This minor masterpiece is the viaduct over the River Ouse near Haversham. Redundant railway workers faced the workhouse and great hardship. Friendly societies helped to alleviate local suffering. Revd Edward Cooke, rector of Haversham, helped to establish Haversham and Castlethorpe Friendly Society in 1811. This held meetings in the church vestry until at least 1846.

General William Booth drives through Stony Stratford on his nationwide tour, 1908. It was a remarkable feat considering that he was eighty and that motor travel was not particularly comfortable. Booth was a Methodist minister before he founded the Salvation Army in 1878.

Salmons' works, 1924. Joseph Salmons started high-class coach building in a small cobbled yard in Tickford Street, Newport Pagnell, in 1820, using local and imported timber. Joseph's grandsons branched out into cars in 1913, and had a display at that year's Olympia Motor Show. The First World War boosted demand for motor cars. The firm concentrated on the luxury market, and became Aston Martin Lagonda in 1953. Miss Salmons of the same family pioneered the cinema in Newport Pagnell.

The pilot of this flimsy aircraft made an emergency landing at Mount Farm, Simpson, between the canal and Watling Street, in 1911. It happened on a Sunday afternoon, when there were plenty of strollers to watch the intrepid young aviator emerge unscathed. (Mount Farm later became an industrial estate.)

Steam tug As161 on the Grand Junction Canal, en route to London, 1914. These boats were built by Hayes of Stony Stratford. Young Edward Hayes came from London in 1840 to establish himself in agricultural engineering. Assisted by William Smith of Woolstone, he responded to orders for motor boats, and went on to specialize in marine engines and vessels which were fit to travel anywhere in the world. As161 ended up working on the River Nile.

The Grand Junction Canal, Great Linford. In 1949 J.H. Peel noted: 'From Willen take the by-lane to Great Linford, leaving a small covert to your right and climbing slowly until at Grange Farm you stand 300 feet above sea level. Thereafter the way crosses a stream. A mile and a half of pleasant going awaits you before this lane crosses the canal and bears right into Great Linford.'

The canal was still busy with working boats when this picture was taken at Great Linford in 1947. The boat on tow was called a 'butty boat', and both vessels may well have been loaded with coal en route for the Buckingham branch. This forked west near Cosgrove, and is now defunct.

Fenny Stratford High Street, 1930s. The Eastern National bus is en route to Stewkley. There is still a lack of cars.

'Nobby Newport' at Great Linford. Peel suggested: 'Your sojourn [here] may be prolonged to coincide with the arrival and subsequent departure of the single line railway.' Muriel Cousins was in charge of this station during the Second World War and remembers the train having to wait on the station while she checked the tickets. 'Sometimes soldiers would get off the last train and I'd walk them up to the camp to show them where it was. You couldn't trust strangers like that today.' Sadly, this track is just a cycleway now.

'Nobby Newport' pauses at Bradwell station, 1959. Goodman's scrapyard is on the left. Before long this old train itself was to join a pile of scrap metal. (B. Brooksbank)

The end of the line for 'Nobby Newport', at Newport Pagnell loco depot, mid-1950s. W.R. Stephens came from London in 1936 and was both driver and fireman on this service. The engines were London & North Western side tanks. The first train left Bletchley at 7.12 a.m. and men waited on a simple wooden platform at what is now Milton Keynes Central, to be taken on to Wolverton. They used to return at 5.45 p.m. (R. Butterfield)

Bradwell scrapyard was sold for housing development in May 1985 to keep the city growing. This interesting item of scrap being cleared out of the yard was an old shunting engine from Scunthorpe steel works. (Pete Sullivan)

Away she goes on a low loader, pulled by a magnificent 6 x 4 Volvo tractor unit. And so the landmark of Goodman's Bradwell scrapyard quickly disappeared. (Pete Sullivan)

Cattle cross the Oxford–Cambridge railway line at Bow Brickhill (about 3 miles from Bletchley), 1948. The name Bow Brickhill derives from the ancient Boel family and the reddish hue of the sandy soils in the hillside.

All is quiet in this Newport Pagnell street, 1948. Sixteen years later Rural District Council chairman Ray Bellchambers aired his Council's views on the South East study to the Town and Country Planning Association: 'We have only given our support because we believe that the city can and should be something which shows that this county can plan, and because we believe this is the way to set the pattern for a new England.'

Stony Stratford High Street, 1950s. At this time it was still part of the old Roman Watling Street (A5) connecting London to the north. New city development and increasing traffic led to the need for a bypass in the early 1970s. The bypass did much to restore the town's old world charm.

Stony Stratford is mentioned in Shakespeare's *Richard III*: 'Last night, I hear they lay at Northampton; At Stony Stratford do they rest tonight: Tomorrow or next day they will be here.' The reference is to King Richard collecting the two princes for the ride to London, and a fate which secured his claim to the throne.

The town had a fine choice of inns fit for royalty. The Cock and the Bull stand close to each other in the High Street. They are monuments to a golden age and provide a clue to the origin of 'cock and bull' stories – easily spun over a long night spent supping strong ale. Perhaps it was such a night, in 1742, when a careless servant at the Bull set fire to washing which was drying by the fire. She thrust blazing linen up the chimney to avoid her mistress's anger and so let loose sparks which set fire to neighbouring thatched houses, St Mary Magdalen Church and farms on either side.

A quiet square in Stony Stratford, 1960s. This end of town looks a little dowdy.

Daily Telegraph news photographer Peter Orme (see p. 69) is seen here at Woburn Ladies Open Championships, October 1984. Peter's awards included first prize in the Canon/UK Press Gazette Images of Sport competition, and he was Courage Central Press's Photographer of the Year in 1985. He has photographed much of the good and bad in city life.

Bletchley railway, looking south-west from the construction site of the new viaduct, 1959. London Brick Company's Bletchley works are visible on the left; at that time they were still in their heyday. By the time Central Milton Keynes Shopping Centre opened, London Brick faced better prospects filling their worked-out clay pits with city rubbish than making bricks.

The viaduct was planned to connect Bletchley with a new marshalling yard at Swanbourne, which was never built. Swanbourne was on the Oxford–Cambridge branch line. This closed to passengers in 1967, and saw only a trickle of goods traffic until 1993. Meanwhile Bletchley main line station received a face-lift in 1966, in preparation for the new city. British Railways' London Midland Region chairman was H.C. Johnson, son of a local farmer from Castlethorpe. He was proud to announce a new car-park for 336 cars on the old engine-shed site and a new electrified service, cutting journey times to 56 minutes. There were also to be important new inter-city connections. (British Railways)

Wolverton Congregational Juniors Football Club (known as the Wolverton Congs), 1935/6 season. Trainer Sam Tuckey is top left and the captain, J. Cooper, is third from the left.

Gathering horses for the battlefields, Market Square, Stony Stratford, *c.* 1915. Soon young men would face similar compulsion in a war that depended on numbers and a great deal of human sacrifice. 'We don't want to lose you, but we think you ought to go' was a popular music-hall lyric of the time.

How young they died. Here are some of the 40,000 troops who arrived over a period at Wolverton for manoeuvres in 1913. Major conflict was a few months away and more youngsters were to volunteer for the glorious conflict – or receive white feathers from certain women who thought carnage a man's lot!

The great struggle over, the survivors of the Bucks Battalion march proudly through the streets of Wolverton, November 1919.

Many families faced the heartbreak of losing loved ones. Here combatants and civilians join in a moment of remembrance, November 1919. The famous lines: 'They shall grow not old, as we that are left grow old: Age shall not weary them, nor the years condemn' give a little comfort.

The parade at Wolverton poignantly meets the children, innocent and hopeful, 1919. They were then the nation's future. Hopes were high. Lloyd George promised 'homes fit for heroes'. Newport Pagnell had started building them and improving water and sewage before the war began.

The war had been for an empire on which the sun could never set, but dreams of a war to end war began to fade by the 1920s. The housing programme slowed. By the 1930s the situation worsened as demand for Britain's traditional exports declined. Wolverton folk managed because they were resourceful and because new local light industries were developing. Inevitably the unemployed, many ex-servicemen, came tramping to these more prosperous areas looking for work. Gwen Brocklehurst remembers to this day the Jarrow Marchers of 1933: 'They came shuffling through Wolverton. The sight affected me very much. Dad came home from Wolverton works and said we had all to go and watch. The little MP Ellen Wilkinson led the men. Jarrow shipyard had no orders and closed. The men were ashen. Some had cloth wrapped round their feet because their soles had worn through. Dad said: "See what happens when men can't find work." They stayed the night at Newport Pagnell workhouse.'

At the same time Hitler was setting the stage for another 'great war'. Oswald Moseley left Labour, to promote the Fascist solution to unemployment. International conflict was inevitable. Palmer's Jarrow shipyard would soon be back in business. There would be plenty of war work to do and more promises of a better future. Post-war planning was to become the new fashion and the hope. The new city of Milton Keynes was on its way.

Jack Cox answered his country's call in 1941 and took his Wolverton works skills to the Royal Air Force. There he worked on the famous Rolls-Royce Merlin engines which powered Spitfires, Hurricanes and Lancasters. He came home briefly to Wolverton in 1942 to marry his childhood sweetheart, Dorothy. He went on to teach apprentices at the works training school, and remembers his time fondly: 'You knew many by sight and many by name. It was more of a family. We did a seven-year apprenticeship and spent two years as improvers.'

Mrs Powell, the village schoolteacher, at Simpson fête, 1948. All the villagers went to the fête during the 1930s and '40s. Baden Powell remembers: 'In 1938 I went in fancy dress as the village pump. I used an old box, lots of brown paper, card and sellotape. My wife went as a knight of the road. [The fête] was on the rectory lawn. She came over to me with a jam jar and pumped the handle. Folk wondered where the water came from! I had a hot water bottle.'

Milford ('Milf') Callow, no. 712, runs past the Old Mill at Wolverton during the annual 5 mile road race, mid-1960s. Milf was paint-shop foreman at the railway works and a linchpin of the athletics club, which was founded in 1885. He remembers the days when it was a struggle to field a cross-country team for the Chiltern League. Now renamed Milton Keynes AC, the club has benefited from the local Mercedes establishment sponsoring an upgraded stadium at Stantonbury; this has an eight-lane track. Club membership is around 500.

Milf Callow and his wife Rose are on the right of this family christening party. Milf met his wife at chapel. She had come up from Wales to teach at Radcliffe School in the 1950s – Wolverton's prosperity attracted many skilled people from far and wide over the years. This picture was taken in Aylesbury Street in 1963. A number of these houses were demolished to make way for the Agora.

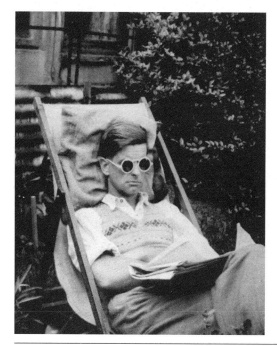

Horace Callow, Milf's father, relaxes in his back garden, late 1940s. His pullover looks very fashionable, but he may have been ahead of his time with the 'John Lennon' sunglasses!

Horace Callow and his wife Winifred at the home of their daughter Joyce, Aylesbury Street, 1963. Horace worked in the finishing shop at the railway works; he also served in the railway fire brigade. The men were very particular about dress in the workplace and ties were a standard item.

Horace and Winifred's children in their back garden, 1941. From left to right: Milford, Joyce, Doreen. Schoolchildren in those days had to learn to live with an influx of youngsters evacuated from the big cities, especially London. Anyone who had space was obliged to accommodate an evacuee. Ironically, two London evacuees were killed when a bomb fell on Bradwell High Street.

Landlord Mr Lovell (wearing an apron) poses with regular at the Greyhound Inn, Haversham, summer 1930.

Mrs Mary Jane Cox, early this century. Her pretty blouse reminds us that hand-made lace had been a local industry. This particular garment seems to be machine made, but this was the machine age, and craft outworkers experienced decline. At one time some men helped their wives with lace making to help scrape a living.

John Cox, the first of three generations to work at Wolverton works this century. His son, known as Jack, remembers his father always going off to work in a traditional flat cap – foremen wore bowlers or trilbies. The works were still expanding then and had engulfed the town's early streets. Gas Street ended up near the coach-frame workshop, and there was a chapel at the stores end near the station. Jack's son John is a foreman fitter and turner in the wheel shop. The recently privatized works need to be 'leaner and fitter' in an age that has seen many local railway services close.

Jack Cox was born and bred in a New Bradwell railway company house. Here, he is home from the war and demonstrating his high-jump skills. His son and daughter both followed his example and became county athletes. To the right, George White relaxes and looks on, after a lifetime in Wolverton works and a distinguished career as a road runner. He participated in the London–Brighton race in the 1920s.

Jack Cox officiates at a walking race, while young Mr Don Tomeni breaks the tape, early 1950s. The park was originally provided by the London & North Western Railway Company for the workers and their families. It was to be used for athletics, cycling and bowls. Haversham bank and a corner of the old works are just visible. This was where the old wooden coaches were broken up.

Schoolboy John Cox wins the
100 yards in 10.6 seconds at the
last Wolverton works sports day,
1960.

Here John Cox has just
finished the Wolverton road
race, 1970. His wife looks
relieved that it's all over. John
came very close to
international standard. Those
were the days before
sponsorship, when a hard
day's work preceded a hard
night's training.

I was definitely the odd man out here. Flower power had got the better of me, making me rather conspicuous among my smart Wolverton Athletic Club colleagues at this trophy presentation at the New Bradwell County Arms, 1969. The others are, standing, left to right: Paul Waring, Paul Absolom, John Reynolds, Steve Adkins. Seated: John Cox, Steve Boreham. The trophies were presented by Lord Cadman of Stoke Goldington.

John 'Josh' Reynolds, like many of the original Wolverton AC members, started work at the railway works. But in the 1960s his trade of riveting and plating became obsolete and he joined Wolverton Post Office Supplies, where he is pictured in 1993. He had been working there for twenty-five years. Asked how his work has changed, he said: 'For years I was a storeman. Now the Post Office has been reorganized I'm called an S0-Stores Operative.'

The R101 airship project was a rival to Barnes Wallis's radically different R100 project. Both were built in twin hangars at Cardington, just a few miles east of the new city area in Bedfordshire. State pride forced the R101 into a maiden voyage to India to beat the R100. However, its gas bags were leaking and it crashed at Beauvais in October 1930. A Bradwell schoolboy carved this memorial to the airship on the little chapel at Bradwell Abbey. The R101 had been a common sight test-flying over the Milton Keynes area and Baden Powell remembers being let out of school to watch it go over.

This little chapel at the former Bradwell Abbey is a reminder of the priory which was founded for Benedictine (Black) monks in about 1155 and dissolved in 1526. The tiny chapel is all that is left of the church, and it has suffered ignoble uses, such as stabling and a carpenter's workshop. Historian and tour guide Ken Powell jokes that the main mistake the monks made was to build it so close to the railway!

The Salvation Army Corps Band at New Bradwell, 1893. The corps used a large upstairs hall at the old mill, which was sold in 1908. In the late nineteenth century officers would be moved on every twelve months.

The Salvation Army Corps Band at New Bradwell, 1926. The standard was high and some bandsmen played in Coventry. The local Salvationist Hall was funded by the local people and the church was sponsored by the railway. Jack and Dorothy Cox remember that the Salvation Army was very important to them. 'It still is, but there's too little support for it so we have to travel to Buckingham,' said Dorothy.

Peel noted in his *Buckinghamshire Footpath* (1949): 'Simpson is not quite so lovely as it was in my boyhood, but it is lovely.' The only virtue he could see in its 1930s Wesleyan chapel was central heating. He generally preferred the older ugly one (p. 83): 'It better suited the simple and narrow piety of the grooms, labourers, farmers and shopkeepers.' Simpson Church, pictured here, had an altar dated 1632, and would have been favoured by the gentry until the social order changed a little in the 1940s.

Fire damage at St Giles' Church in Stony Stratford High Street, early 1970s. God moves in mysterious ways and perhaps nothing is, or ever was, sacred!

Acknowledgements

It is impossible to measure the relative importance of all the contributions to this book. Everyone listed below provided something which I felt was very important – whether pictures, notes or anecdotes. In many cases particular contributions are obvious from the captions or the credits. Not so obvious is the part played by Ray Bellchambers in going over so much of the development history of Milton Keynes, or Brian O'Sullivan's guidance on technical details of construction, backed up by a wealth of pictures.

All reasonable efforts have been made to trace copyright holders. I wish to thank everyone who helped me, and I hope I have not forgotten anyone.

Barbara and Bill Barton • Ray Bellchambers • Bill Billings • Gwen Blane
Martin Blane • Bradwell Abbey – Ken Powell • British Railways
B. Brooksbank • Bucks County Fire and Rescue • R. Butterfield • Milf Callow
Rose Callow • Central Milton Keynes Shopping Centre
Commission for New Towns, Milton Keynes • Nicola Cook
County Library – Jane Cutler and Julian Hunt • Muriel Cousins
Dorothy Cox • John Cox • Jack Cox • John Crook
De Montfort University – Simon Malcolm and Pat Parkhurst
Elizabeth Eastham and Mike Eastham • Jeffrey Goddard • Gwen Harris
MADCAP Trust – Phillipa Tipper
Milton Keynes City Orchestra – Katherine Turvey
Museum of Rural Life – Stacey Bushes and Bill Griffiths
Open University – Debbie Nicholls • Helen Osborne • Brian O'Sullivan
Peter Orme • Andy Powell • Baden Powell • Radcliffe School • John Reynolds
Colin Stacey • Jenny Stacey • Stantonbury Campus • Robert Storer
Pete Sullivan • Thames Valley Police • Mike Thomas • Volkswagen AG
Willen Hospice • Woodhill Prison

BRITAIN IN OLD PHOTOGRAPHS

To order any of these titles please telephone Littlehampton Book Services on 01903 721596

ALDERNEY

Alderney: A Second Selection, *B Bonnard*

BEDFORDSHIRE

Bedfordshire at Work, *N Lutt*

BERKSHIRE

Maidenhead, *M Hayles & D Hedges*
Around Maidenhead, *M Hayles & B Hedges*
Reading, *P Southerton*
Reading: A Second Selection, *P Southerton*
Sandhurst and Crowthorne, *K Dancy*
Around Slough, *J Hunter & K Hunter*
Around Thatcham, *P Allen*
Around Windsor, *B Hedges*

BUCKINGHAMSHIRE

Buckingham and District, *R Cook*
High Wycombe, *R Goodearl*
Around Stony Stratford, *A Lambert*

CHESHIRE

Cheshire Railways, *M Hitches*
Chester, *S Nichols*

CLWYD

Clwyd Railways, *M Hitches*

CLYDESDALE

Clydesdale, *Lesmahagow Parish Historical Association*

CORNWALL

Cornish Coast, *T Bowden*
Falmouth, *P Gilson*
Lower Fal, *P Gilson*
Around Padstow, *M McCarthy*
Around Penzance, *J Holmes*
Penzance and Newlyn, *J Holmes*
Around Truro, *A Lyne*
Upper Fal, *P Gilson*

CUMBERLAND

Cockermouth and District, *J Bernard Bradbury*
Keswick and the Central Lakes, *J Marsh*
Around Penrith, *F Boyd*
Around Whitehaven, *H Fancy*

DERBYSHIRE

Derby, *D Buxton*
Around Matlock, *D Barton*

DEVON

Colyton and Seaton, *T Gosling*
Dawlish and Teignmouth, *G Gosling*
Devon Aerodromes, *K Saunders*
Exeter, *P Thomas*
Exmouth and Budleigh Salterton, *T Gosling*
From Haldon to Mid-Dartmoor, *T Hall*
Honiton and the Otter Valley, *J Yallop*
Around Kingsbridge, *K Tanner*
Around Seaton and Sidmouth, *T Gosling*
Seaton, Axminster and Lyme Regis, *T Gosling*

DORSET

Around Blandford Forum, *B Cox*
Bournemouth, *M Colman*
Bridport and the Bride Valley, *J Burrell & S Humphries*
Dorchester, *T Gosling*
Around Gillingham, *P Crocker*

DURHAM

Darlington, *G Flynn*
Darlington: A Second Selection, *G Flynn*
Durham People, *M Richardson*
Houghton-le-Spring and Hetton-le-Hole, *K Richardson*
Houghton-le-Spring and Hetton-le-Hole:
   A Second Selection, *K Richardson*
Sunderland, *S Miller & B Bell*
Teesdale, *D Coggins*
Teesdale: A Second Selection, *P Raine*
Weardale, *J Crosby*
Weardale: A Second Selection, *J Crosby*

DYFED

Aberystwyth and North Ceredigion,
   Dyfed Cultural Services Dept
Haverfordwest, *Dyfed Cultural Services Dept*
Upper Tywi Valley, *Dyfed Cultural Services Dept*

ESSEX

Around Grays, *B Evans*

GLOUCESTERSHIRE

Along the Avon from Stratford to Tewkesbury, *J Jeremiah*
Cheltenham: A Second Selection, *R Whiting*
Cheltenham at War, *P Gill*
Cirencester, *J Welsford*
Around Cirencester, *E Cuss & P Griffiths*
Forest, The, *D Mullin*
Gloucester, *J Voyce*
Around Gloucester, *A Sutton*
Gloucester: From the Walwin Collection, *J Voyce*
North Cotswolds, *D Viner*
Severn Vale, *A Sutton*
Stonehouse to Painswick, *A Sutton*
Stroud and the Five Valleys, *S Gardiner & L Padin*
Stroud and the Five Valleys: A Second Selection,
   S Gardiner & L Padin
Stroud's Golden Valley, *S Gardiner & L Padin*
Stroudwater and Thames & Severn Canals,
   E Cuss & S Gardiner
Stroudwater and Thames & Severn Canals: A Second
   Selection, *E Cuss & S Gardiner*
Tewkesbury and the Vale of Gloucester, *C Hilton*
Thornbury to Berkeley, *J Hudson*
Uley, Dursley and Cam, *A Sutton*
Wotton-under-Edge to Chipping Sodbury, *A Sutton*

GWYNEDD

Anglesey, *M Hitches*
Gwynedd Railways, *M Hitches*
Around Llandudno, *M Hitches*
Vale of Conwy, *M Hitches*

HAMPSHIRE

Gosport, *J Sadden*
Portsmouth, *P Rogers & D Francis*

HEREFORDSHIRE

Herefordshire, *A Sandford*

HERTFORDSHIRE

Barnet, *I Norrie*
Hitchin, *A Fleck*
St Albans, *S Mullins*
Stevenage, *M Appleton*

ISLE OF MAN

The Tourist Trophy, *B Snelling*

ISLE OF WIGHT

Newport, *D Parr*
Around Ryde, *D Parr*

JERSEY

Jersey: A Third Selection, *R Lemprière*

KENT

Bexley, *M Scott*
Broadstairs and St Peter's, *J Whyman*
Bromley, Keston and Hayes, *M Scott*
Canterbury: A Second Selection, *D Butler*
Chatham and Gillingham, *P MacDougall*
Chatham Dockyard, *P MacDougall*
Deal, *J Broady*
Early Broadstairs and St Peter's, *B Wootton*
East Kent at War, *D Collyer*
Eltham, *J Kennett*
Folkestone: A Second Selection, *A Taylor & E Rooney*
Goudhurst to Tenterden, *A Guilmant*
Gravesend, *R Hiscock*
Around Gravesham, *R Hiscock & D Grierson*
Herne Bay, *J Hawkins*
Lympne Airport, *D Collyer*
Maidstone, *I Hales*
Margate, *R Clements*
RAF Hawkinge, *R Humphreys*
RAF Manston, *RAF Manston History Club*
RAF Manston: A Second Selection,
   RAF Manston History Club
Ramsgate and Thanet Life, *D Perkins*
Romney Marsh, *E Carpenter*
Sandwich, *C Wanostrocht*
Around Tonbridge, *C Bell*
Tunbridge Wells, *M Rowlands & I Beavis*
Tunbridge Wells: A Second Selection,
   M Rowlands & I Beavis
Around Whitstable, *C Court*
Wingham, Adisham and Littlebourne, *M Crane*

LANCASHIRE

Around Barrow-in-Furness, *J Garbutt & J Marsh*
Blackpool, *C Rothwell*
Bury, *J Hudson*
Chorley and District, *J Smith*
Fleetwood, *C Rothwell*
Heywood, *J Hudson*
Around Kirkham, *C Rothwell*
Lancashire North of the Sands, *J Garbutt & J Marsh*
Around Lancaster, *S Ashworth*
Lytham St Anne's, *C Rothwell*
North Fylde, *C Rothwell*
Radcliffe, *J Hudson*
Rossendale, *B Moore & N Dunnachie*

LEICESTERSHIRE

Around Ashby-de-la-Zouch, *K Hillier*
Charnwood Forest, *I Keil, W Humphrey & D Wix*
Leicester, *D Burton*
Leicester: A Second Selection, *D Burton*
Melton Mowbray, *T Hickman*
Around Melton Mowbray, *T Hickman*
River Soar, *D Wix, P Shacklock & I Keil*
Rutland, *T Clough*
Vale of Belvoir, *T Hickman*
Around the Welland Valley, *S Mastoris*

LINCOLNSHIRE

Grimsby, *J Tierney*
Around Grimsby, *J Tierney*
Grimsby Docks, *J Tierney*
Lincoln, *D Cuppleditch*

Scunthorpe, *D Taylor*
Skegness, *W Kime*
Around Skegness, *W Kime*

LONDON

Balham and Tooting, *P Loobey*
Crystal Palace, Penge & Anerley, *M Scott*
Greenwich and Woolwich, *K Clark*
Hackney: A Second Selection, *D Mander*
Lewisham and Deptford, *J Coulter*
Lewisham and Deptford: A Second Selection, *J Coulter*
Streatham, *P Loobey*
Around Whetstone and North Finchley, *J Heathfield*
Woolwich, *B Evans*

MONMOUTHSHIRE

Chepstow and the River Wye, *A Rainsbury*
Monmouth and the River Wye, *Monmouth Museum*

NORFOLK

Great Yarmouth, *M Teun*
Norwich, *M Colman*
Wymondham and Attleborough, *P Yaxley*

NORTHAMPTONSHIRE

Around Stony Stratford, *A Lambert*

NOTTINGHAMSHIRE

Arnold and Bestwood, *M Spick*
Arnold and Bestwood: A Second Selection, *M Spick*
Changing Face of Nottingham, *G Oldfield*
Mansfield, *Old Mansfield Society*
Around Newark, *T Warner*
Nottingham: 1944–1974, *D Whitworth*
Sherwood Forest, *D Ottewell*
Victorian Nottingham, *M Payne*

OXFORDSHIRE

Around Abingdon, *P Horn*
Banburyshire, *M Barnett & S Gosling*
Burford, *A Jewell*
Around Didcot and the Hagbournes, *B Lingham*
Garsington, *M Gunther*
Around Henley-on-Thames, *S Ellis*
Oxford: The University, *J Rhodes*
Thame to Watlington, *N Hood*
Around Wallingford, *D Beasley*
Witney, *T Worley*
Around Witney, *C Mitchell*
Witney District, *T Worley*
Around Woodstock, *J Bond*

POWYS

Brecon, *Brecknock Museum*
Welshpool, *E Bredsdorff*

SHROPSHIRE

Shrewsbury, *D Trumper*
Whitchurch to Market Drayton, *M Morris*

SOMERSET

Bath, *J Hudson*
Bridgwater and the River Parrett, *R Fitzhugh*
Bristol, *D Moorcroft & N Campbell-Sharp*
Changing Face of Keynsham,
   B Lowe & M Whitehead

Chard and Ilminster, *G Gosling & F Huddy*
Crewkerne and the Ham Stone Village's,
   G Gosling & F Huddy
Around Keynsham and Saltford, *B Lowe & T Brown*
Midsomer Norton and Radstock, *C Howell*
Somerton, Ilchester and Langport, *G Gosling & F Huddy*
Taunton, *N Chipchase*
Around Taunton, *N Chipchase*
Wells, *C Howell*
Weston-Super-Mare, *S Poole*
Around Weston-Super-Mare, *S Poole*
West Somerset Villages, *K Houghton & L Thomas*

STAFFORDSHIRE

Aldridge, *J Farrow*
Bilston, *E Rees*
Black Country Transport: Aviation, *A Brew*
Around Burton upon Trent, *G Sowerby & R Farman*
Bushbury, *A Chatwin, M Mills & E Rees*
Around Cannock, *M Mills & S Belcher*
Around Leek, *R Poole*
Lichfield, *H Clayton & K Simmons*
Around Pattingham and Wombourne, *M Griffiths,*
   P Leigh & M Mills
Around Rugeley, *T Randall & J Anslow*
Smethwick, *J Maddison*
Stafford, *J Anslow & T Randall*
Around Stafford, *J Anslow & T Randall*
Stoke-on-Trent, *I Lawley*
Around Tamworth, *R Sulima*
Around Tettenhall and Codsall, *M Mills*
Tipton, Wednesbury and Darlaston, *R Pearson*
Walsall, *D Gilbert & M Lewis*
Wednesbury, *I Bott*
West Bromwich, *R Pearson*

SUFFOLK

Ipswich: A Second Selection, *D Kindred*
Around Ipswich, *D Kindred*
Around Mildenhall, *C Dring*
Southwold to Aldeburgh, *H Phelps*
Around Woodbridge, *H Phelps*

SURREY

Cheam and Belmont, *P Berry*
Croydon, *S Bligh*
Dorking and District, *K Harding*
Around Dorking, *A Jackson*
Around Epsom, *P Berry*
Farnham: A Second Selection, *J Parratt*
Around Haslemere and Hindhead, *T Winter & G Collyer*
Richmond, *Richmond Local History Society*
Sutton, *P Berry*

SUSSEX

Arundel and the Arun Valley, *J Godfrey*
Bishopstone and Seaford, *P Pople & P Berry*
Brighton and Hove, *J Middleton*
Brighton and Hove: A Second Selection, *J Middleton*
Around Crawley, *M Goldsmith*
Hastings, *P Haines*
Hastings: A Second Selection, *P Haines*
Around Haywards Heath, *J Middleton*
Around Heathfield, *A Gillet & B Russell*
Around Heathfield: A Second Selection,
   A Gillet & B Russell
High Weald, *B Harwood*
High Weald: A Second Selection, *B Harwood*
Horsham and District, *T Wales*

Lewes, *J Middleton*
RAF Tangmere, *A Saunders*
Around Rye, *A Dickinson*
Around Worthing, *S White*

WARWICKSHIRE

Along the Avon from Stratford to Tewkesbury, *J Jeremiah*
Bedworth, *J Burton*
Coventry, *D McGrory*
Around Coventry, *D McGrory*
Nuneaton, *S Clews & S Vaughan*
Around Royal Leamington Spa, *J Cameron*
Around Royal Leamington Spa: A Second Selection,
   J Cameron
Around Warwick, *R Booth*

WESTMORLAND

Eden Valley, *J Marsh*
Kendal, *M & P Duff*
South Westmorland Villages, *J Marsh*
Westmorland Lakes, *J Marsh*

WILTSHIRE

Around Amesbury, *P Daniels*
Chippenham and Lacock, *A Wilson & M Wilson*
Around Corsham and Box, *A Wilson & M Wilson*
Around Devizes, *D Buxton*
Around Highworth, *G Tanner*
Around Highworth and Faringdon, *G Tanner*
Around Malmesbury, *A Wilson*
Marlborough: A Second Selection, *P Colman*
Around Melksham,
   Melksham and District Historical Association
Nadder Valley, *R. Sawyer*
Salisbury, *P Saunders*
Salisbury: A Second Selection, *P Daniels*
Salisbury: A Third Selection, *P Daniels*
Around Salisbury, *P Daniels*
Swindon: A Third Selection, *The Swindon Society*
Swindon: A Fourth Selection, *The Swindon Society*
Trowbridge, *M Marshman*
Around Wilton, *P Daniels*
Around Wootton Bassett, Cricklade and Purton, *T Sharp*

WORCESTERSHIRE

Evesham to Bredon, *F Archer*
Around Malvern, *K Smith*
Around Pershore, *M Dowty*
Redditch and the Needle District, *R Saunders*
Redditch: A Second Selection, *R Saunders*
Around Tenbury Wells, *D Green*
Worcester, *M Dowty*
Around Worcester, *R Jones*
Worcester in a Day, *M Dowty*
Worcestershire at Work, *R Jones*

YORKSHIRE

Huddersfield: A Second Selection, *H Wheeler*
Huddersfield: A Third Selection, *H Wheeler*
Leeds Road and Rail, *R Vickers*
Pontefract, *R van Riel*
Scarborough, *D Coggins*
Scarborough's War Years, *R Percy*
Skipton and the Dales, *Friends of the Craven Museum*
Around Skipton-in-Craven, *Friends of the Craven Museum*
Yorkshire Wolds, *I & M Sumner*